AF697406

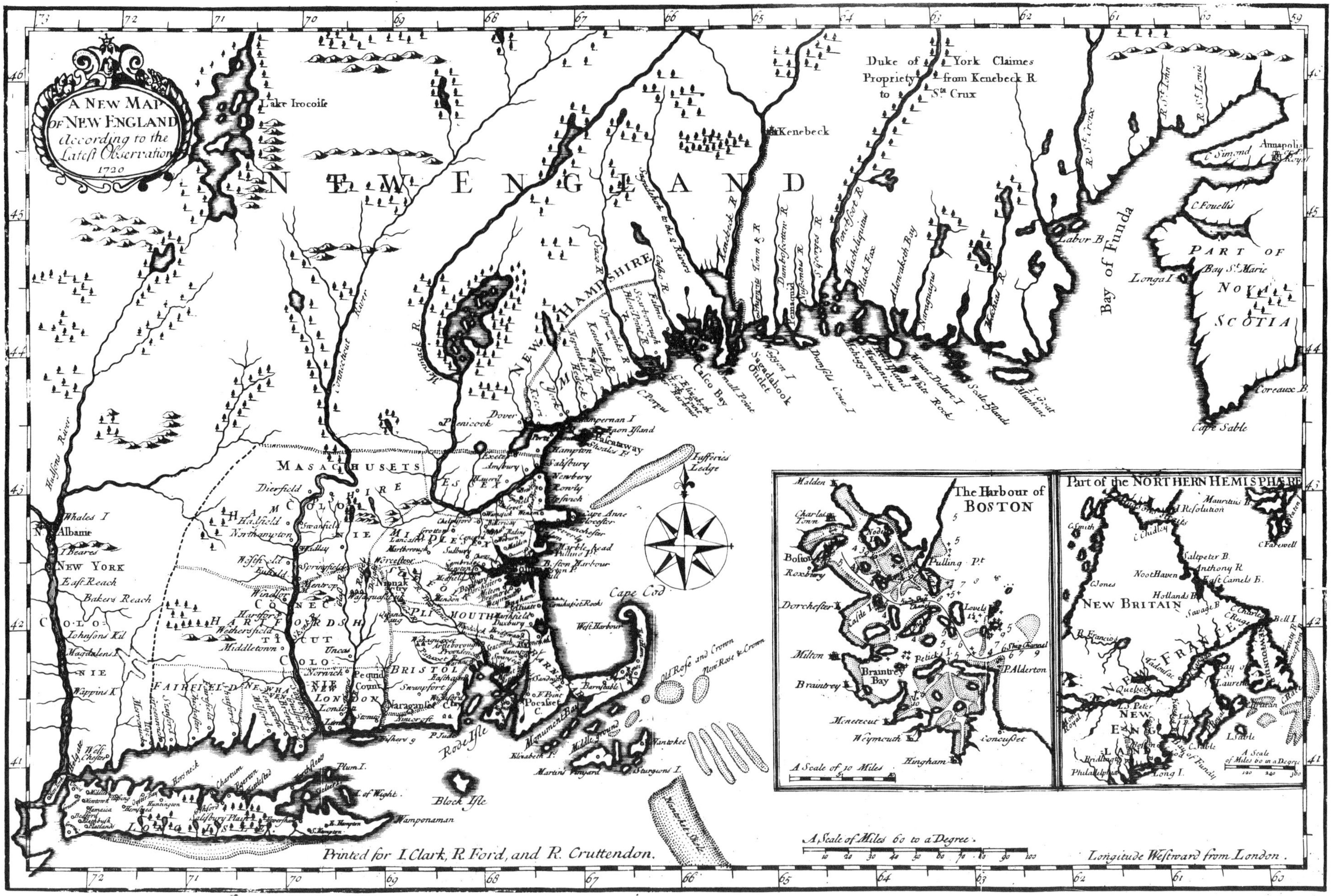
A NEW MAP OF NEW ENGLAND according to the Latest Observation 1720
NEW ENGLAND
NEW HAMPSHIRE
MASACHUSETS COLONIE
NEW YORK
HARTFORDSHIRE
CONECTICUT COLONIE
NEW LONDON
BRISTOL
PLIMOUTH
PART OF NOVA SCOTIA
Bay of Funda
Duke of York Claimes Propriety from Kenebeck R to Sta Crux
Kenebeck
Annapolis Royal
Cape Sable
Lake Irocoise
Hudsons River
Albanie
Boston
Casco Bay
Cape Anne
Cape Cod
Block Isle
Rode Isle
Jefferies Ledge
The Harbour of BOSTON
Malden
Charlestown
Roxbury
Dorchester
Milton
Braintrey
Braintrey Bay
Pulling Pt
Weymouth
Hingham
Concusset
P. Alderton
A Scale of 10 Miles
Part of the NORTHERN HEMISPHÆRE
NEW BRITAIN
NEW FRANCE
NEW ENGLAND
Quebec
Philadelphia
Long I.
A Scale of Miles 60 to a Degree
Printed for I. Clark, R. Ford, and R. Cruttendon.
A Scale of Miles 60 to a Degree.
Longitude Westward from London.

THE

LAWS OF NEW ENGLAND

TO THE YEAR

1700

Opposite: Folding Map of New England in 1720

THE

LAWS OF NEW ENGLAND

TO THE YEAR

1700

Middlebury, Connecticut

THE CARROLLTON PRESS

MCMXCI

All Rights Reserved

1991

First Printing

ISBN # 0-9627424-0-6

Cover illustration by Rosanna Pacilio

Printed in the United States of America

INTRODUCTION

The following pages contain an abridgement of the laws and ordinances of New England up to the year 1700. They have been faithfully reproduced from one of the earliest printed histories of New England-*The History of New England Containing an Impartial Account of the Civil and Ecclesiastical Affairs of the Country to the Year of Our Lord, 1700.* This work was originally published in London in 1720 by the English clergyman Daniel Neal.

In this summary are laws affecting everyday life in the earliest decades of Colonial America. Covering areas of concern from minor infractions and civil matters to capital offenses and the administration of the militia, the laws and punishments are simple and straight forward. Included are laws relating to **Galloping Horses** (no one to gallop a horse in Boston), **Spinning** (all hands not employ'd are oblig'd to spin), **Wages** (which may be paid in corn), and **Witches** (they suffer death). Other topics addressed include Children, Courtship & Marriage, Currency, Farming, Fishing, Gaming, Heresy, Indians, Prisons and Punishments, Publick Houses, Smoking, Tryals, Ships & Wharfage, etc.

This compendium of early laws is both interesting and informative, providing insight into the early origins of the American legal system.

© THE CARROLLTON PRESS, 1991.

An Abridgment of the Laws, and Ordinances of New-England, *to the Year* 1700.

A.

ACtions, Actions of Debts, Accounts, Slander, Actions of the caſe concerning Debts or Accounts, the Plaintiff may try where he will within the Juriſdiction of the Court, where he or the Defendant lives; by conſent, they may be try'd any where elſe. Other Actions muſt be try'd where the Cauſe did ariſe.

If the Plaintiff in an Action of Treſpaſs pretends Damage above 40 *s*, and has receiv'd leſs, he ſhall be Non-ſuited, and pay Coſts.

No Action to be enter'd after the firſt Day of the Court's ſitting. Double Fees, for thoſe enter'd after Noon not to be recover'd of the Defendant.

Who-

Whoever brings an Action without cauſe, muſt pay the charges the Court ſhall judge he occaſion'd, and any Fine they impoſe; as likewiſe the Defendant, if they find him in Fault; Vexatious Actions, or Suits, to pay treble coſts, and to be fin'd 40*s.* to the Treaſury.

Adultery. If any Perſon commit Adultery with a marry'd Woman, Maid, or Woman eſpouſed, both Man and Woman ſhall be put to Death.

Age. No Perſon under 21 Years of Age, ſhall convey Lands or Hereditaments, or val in Eleccons of publick Offices, or give Verdict, or paſs Sentence in any civil or criminal Court, or cauſe.

Orphans may chooſe their Guardians at 14.

None under the Age of 21, ſhall plead, or be impleaded in civil caſes, but in the Names of their Parents, Maſters, or Guardians.

But in criminal caſes, they muſt anſwer for their Miſdemeanours, and inform againſt others in their owu Names.

Apparel. All Perſons not worth 200*l.* wearing Gold or Silver Lace, or Buttons, or Bone-Lace, above 2*s.* *per* Yard, or Silk Hoods, or Scarfs, may be preſented by the Grand-Jury, and ſhall pay 10*s.* for every Offence.

The ſelect Men of every Town may aſſeſs thoſe who dreſs above their Rank, at 200*l.* Eſtate, and make them pay, as thoſe to whom their Dreſs is ſuitable, except Magiſtrates, their Wives, and Children, Officers, civil or military, Soldiers in Time of Service; or ſuch as have had a high Education, or are ſunk from a higher Fortune, *Anno* 1651.

If any Perſon's Dreſs ſhould be adjudg'd by theGrand Jury, or County-Court above his Rank, they are to be admoniſh'd for the firſt Offence, to pay 20*s.* for the ſecond, 40*s.* for the third, and 40*s.* for every Offence afterwards, *Anno* 1662,

A Taylor who makes Cloaths for Children, or Servants, contrary to the Mind of their Parents or Maſters, is for the firſt Offence, to be admoniſhed, and for the ſecond, to pay double the Value of the Cloaths, half to the Owner, and half to the County, 1662. The Grand-Jury are enjoin'd to preſent all Offenders in Apparel. *Ibid.* Ap-

Appeal. Any Perſon may appeal from an inferior to a ſuperior Court, provided they tender their Appeal before the Judges of the Court they appeal to, put in Bail to proſecute it, and to pay Damages before Execution, which can't be 'till 12 Hours after Judgment, unleſs by ſpecial Order.

Appellants in criminal caſes to give Security for Appearance and good Behaviour.

Appeals in Matter of Law, to be determin'd by the Bench; in Matter of Fact, by Bench and Jury.

In an Appeal to the Court of Aſſiſtants in any capital Offence, if two in five, or three in ſeven, or the like Proportion diſſent from the Majority, there lyes an Appeal to the next General Court.

Appeals to be recorded at the charge of the Appellant, and certified to the Court to which they are made, the Reaſons of them, without any Reflecting Language, to be given in Writing under their Hands, or their Attorney's Hands, to the Clerk of the Court from whence they are made, ſix Days before the Court begins to which they are made.

Appellants not proſecuting their Appeals, to pay, beſide their Bonds to the Party, 40 *s.* to the County.

No Perſon who ſate as Judge, or voted in the inferiour Court, ſhall have a Vote in that Court to which the Appeal is made in the ſame caſe, but it ſhall be decided by different Perſons.

The Court appeal'd to, ſhall judge the caſe according to the former Evidence, and no other Court may reverſe Judgment, or abate, or increaſe Damages, *Anno* 1654.

Appeals from the Aſſociation-Courts of *Portſmouth* and *Dover*, are to the next County Court, and not to that of Aſſiſtants at *Boſton*, as formerly, *Anno* 1670.

Appearance. No one to be puniſh'd for Non-Appearance, if hinder'd by Providence. This Law not to prejudice any Perſon in his coſts or damages in civil Actions, *Anno* 1641.

Arreſts. None to be arreſted, or put in Priſon for Debt, if the Law finds any Means of Satisfaction from his Eſtate, except in ſpecial contracts, *Anno* 1641.

The Perſon arreſted to be in Priſon at his own charge, unleſs the Court determine otherwiſe, but not to continue there, unleſs there is an Appearance of ſome Eſtate conceal'd, *Anno* 1641.

The

The Prisoner swearing before a proper Magistrate that he has no Estate, is to be releas'd, but is to make Satisfaction by Service, though not to be sold to any besides the *English*, *Anno* 1647.

In civil Actions, the Prisoner swearing he is not worth 5 *l.* the Plaintiff must maintain him in Prison, levying by Execution his Expence, if he can find Effects.

No Prisoner to go at Liberty, without License of the Court, or Creditor, if he does, the Keeper to be fin'd at Discretion, and pay the Debt.

Attachments. A Foreigner can't attach an Inhabitant, without giving Security to prosecute his Account, and pay costs, if cast.

The Suit not to proceed, unless legal Notice be given of Attachments of Goods, or Lands, by writing left at the Place of Abode of the Defendant.

If the Defendant be out of the Jurisdiction of the Court where the Attachment lyes, the cause goes on, but Judgment is not to be enter'd 'till the next Court, nor Execution granted, 'till the Plaintiff gives Security to the Defendant to be responsible, in case he reverses Judgment within a Year, or such longer Time as the Court directs.

If the Plaintiff does not express in whose Name or capacity he sueth, Exception may be taken, and the Plaintiff must pay costs.

Tho' the Law directs the Attachment to Constables, where no Marshal lives, yet a Marshal may serve it any where in the Jurisdiction of the Court where he is an Officer, but he is to be paid no more than a Constable, *Anno* 1662.

B.

Bakers, see Bread.

Ballast. No Ballast to be taken out of any Town, Slough, without Leave of the select Men, under Penalty of 6 *d.* a Shovel-full, except it be what they laid there themselves.

No Ballast to be cast out to the Prejudice of any Harbour, under Penalty of 10 *s.* *Anno* 1646.

Bar-

Barratry. The Court may reject the Cause of a common Barrater, that vexes others with unjust Suits, and may punish him for his Barratry, 1641.

Bastardy. The Father of a Bastard convict shall maintain it, or allow the Mother what the Court thinks fit.

The Oath of the Woman alone makes him liable to this charge, though not to any Punishment due by the Law in cases of Fornication and Adultery; but if circumstances render the Fact doubtful, the Court may acquit him.

Bestiality. If a Man or Woman lye with a Beast, the Beast to be slain and buried, and the Person put to Death.

Benevolence. No Benevolence to be granted, but in foreign Occasions, and when publick Debts are paid, and there is Money in the Treasury.

The County-Court may take Notice of Gifts and Legacies to publick Uses, and if they see cause, may appoint Feoffees of Trust to settle and manage them.

Bills Assigned. Bills, or other Specialties may be assigned, and the Right of Account shall be in the Assignee, so that he may sue for them in his own Name, or by Attorney, provided the Assignment be indors'd on the Back of the Bill.

Blasphemy. Blasphemy against the Holy Name of God, the Father, Son, or Holy Ghost, either in express Words, or by an obstinate Denial of the true God and his Worship, shall be punish'd with Death.

Bond-Men. None to be bought, or sold for Slaves but those who are taken in War, or made such by Authority, and these to have the same Liberties, as those under the Law of *Moses*.

Bounds of Lands. The Bounds of every Town are to be set out within a Year after they are granted.

The Marks of those Bounds to be renew'd every three Years, by three, or more Inhabitants chosen by the select Men, who together with the adjacent Towns, shall go the Bounds, and renew the Land-Marks.

The Time for this must be in the first or second Month; Notice to be given of it by the most ancient Town; the Bounds must be a Heap of Stones, or a Trench.

The

The Town that neglects to renew them ſhall forfeit 5 *l.* The Men appointed for this to be under the Direction of the ſelect Men, and paid by the Towns.

Thoſe who have Lands in common, muſt viſit their Bounds once a Year, or pay 10*s.* for every Day they neglect it after they are requeſted to do ſo.

Breach of the Peace. If one Man beats or hurts another, he ſhall pay to him, or the County, or both, what the proper Judge determines, who may fine him according to the circumſtances of the Offence.

To keep Poſſeſſion of any Thing, or to endeavour to regain it by Force after Execution upon Judgment obtain'd, is a Breach of the Peace; the Officers of Juſtice are to aid the Plaintiff, and commit the Offender and his Abettors, who are to anſwer for it at the Court where the Judgment was obtain'd, and to be puniſh'd as the Court thinks fit.

Bread. The Baker is to mark his Bread, and to make it up according to the following Aſſizes.

When Wheat is at

s.	*d.*		White. *Ou.*	White. *qr.*	Wheat. *Ou.*	Wheat. *qr.*	Houſhold. *Ou.*	Houſhold. *qr.*
3	0	per Buſhel, each Penny-Loaf muſt weigh	11	1	17	1	23	0
3	6		10	1	15	1	20	2
4	0		9	1	14	0	18	2
4	6		8	1	11	3	16	2
5	0		7	3	11	2	15	2
5	6		7	0	10	2	14	0
6	0		6	2	11	0	13	0
6	6		6	0	9	2	11	2

Two Perſons in every Market-Town choſen annually, and ſworn at the next County-Court, or neareſt Magiſtrate, have Power with, or without a Conſtable, to enter any Houſe where they are inform'd that Bread is made for Sale, and weigh the Bread, and ſeize what is under Weight, a Third for themſelves, and the reſt for the Poor.

Brewers. None may brew for Sale or Shipping, but ſuch as are known to be ſkilful in that Art.

If the Beer they ſell for Sea proves unfit for Uſe, through their Fault, Damages may be recover'd of them by Action.

Bridges.

Bridges. Bridges to be made in ſuch Places, and repair'd, as the County-Court, or a Committee appointed by them directs, at the charge of the County, to be levy'd upon the Towns according to the County Rates.

If any Bridge or Highway be defective, and any Perſon in paſſing it loſe his Life, after legal Preſentment of it to the County-Court, the County or Town ſhall pay 100 *l.* to the neareſt Relation of the Deceaſed.

If any Perſon loſe a Limb, break a Bone, or receive a Bruiſe, or if any Damage happen to any Team, or their Lading, the Party may recover double Damages, if due Notice have been given, as before.

Any Magiſtrate may iſſue out Warrants to Conſtables, to preſs Men, Horſes, or Carts, for repairing a Bridge or High-way, who ſhall be paid for their Work by ſuch Towns, or Perſons to whom the Bridge belongs.

Burgeſſes. Burgeſſes muſt be Members of ſome Church, gathered by conſent of the Eſtabliſh'd Churches of the Country.

They may chooſe out of their Body ordinary Judges of their ſeveral Towns, and Deputies, who join'd with the Governour and his Aſſiſtants, conſtitute the General Court.

Burglary and Robbery. Burglary and Robbery on the Highway ſhall be puniſh'd for the firſt Offence, with burning in the Forehead, with the Letter *B*: and the Loſs of an Ear, if on the Sabbath; for the ſecond, with Burning and Whipping; and the Loſs of t'other Ear, if on the Sabbath; for the third, with Death.

C.

Cask. All Cask to be of *London* Aſſize, and of good Timber, to be gaug'd, and mark'd by Gaugers, who are to have 4 *d. per* Ton.

Every Cooper that ſets not his Mark on his Cask, to pay 20 *s.*

Bad Cask expos'd to Sale forfeited to the Informer, and the Owner to be fin'd 10 *s. per* Ton.

A Gauger to be choſen, and ſworn annually, and to pay 40 *s.* if he refuſes to officiate; the Town that neglects to chuſe one, forfeits 40 *s.*

The

The Gauger is to fee that Goods are pack'd in Casks of true Affize, and to pay 10 *s.* for every defective Cask, half to the Informer, and half to the County.

He is alfo to view Victuals, and to receive 4 *s.* *per* Ton, if 'tis defective, if otherwife, but one.

All Goods expos'd to Sale without the Gauger's Mark forfeited, half to the Informer, half to the County.

Hogfhead-Staves are to be 3 Foot 2 Inches in Length, Barrel-Staves 31 Inches, Heading for Pipe-Staves 28 Inches in Length, and for Hogfheads and Barrels fuitable to the Staves.

Cattle. The Cattle of every Town muft be mark'd with a diftinct Mark, or pay double Damage, if they trefpafs.

The Mark of fuch Cattle as feed in open common without Keeper to be on the Shoulder, or home left Buttock, and the Clerk of the Writs in every Town to keep a Copy of the Marks.

No unruly Beaft to feed in common, or Ground next to Corn-Fields, or any fenced Ground without Fetters.

The Party aggriev'd by Trefpafs, may bring his Action, or refer his Damage to two Neighbours, which the Owner of the Beaft fhall pay.

But if he difapproves of the Judgment, the Parties by confent may nominate each of them a Man to review the Damage, who may fet afide the former Judgment, provided they agree upon it the fame Day.

Cattle taken in another's Ground may be impounded, 'till Notice given to their Owner, who may replevy them, or the other may return them, and bring his Action.

In cafe of involuntary Trefpafs, the Trefpaffer tendring full Damage before Suit commenced, fhall not pay Cofts, though the other fues him.

Whoever receives Damage from Cattle by his own Fault, fhall recover nothing.

If Goats damage any one, the Owner fhall pay double Damage, and the Perfon damnify'd fhall keep and milk them 'till he has receiv'd Satisfaction.

Whoever takes another's Beaft, and works it without Leave, fhall pay treble Damages, or 10 *s.* if the Plaintiff demands it; if they can't pay it, they fhall be otherwife punifh'd, as the Magiftrate fees caufe.

Drift

Drift Cattle may be fed in any open Land, not appropriated to any Ufe.

Charges of the publick. No Governour, Deputy-Governour, Affiftant, Affociate, Grand or Petty Juryman, Deputy for the General Court, or Commiffioner for military Difcipline, fhall ferve the Publick at their own Expence.

Every Perfon to be affeffed by the Country Rates for all Charges in Church and State, their Lands in the Towns where they lye, and their Perfons where they dwell. The Money to be levy'd on Defaulters by Diftrefs: If nothing is found, they are to be imprifon'd 'till the County Court, or 'till Security given.

The Treafurer every *July* fhall fend his Warrant to the Conftables of every Town, to fummon the Inhabitants to chufe a Commiffioner for Affeffments, who with the felect Men fhall in *Auguft* take a Lift of all male Perfons above fixteen, and a Survey of their Eftates, and affefs them 20 *d. per* Head, (except Magiftrates, and Elders of Churches), and their Eftates at a Penny *per* Pound.

The Eftates of Traders are to be rated at the Difcretion of the Affeffors, but they may complain, if overrated, to the General Court. None to pay for Lands in *England*.

A Bull or Cow of 4 Years old, is to be rated at 3 *l.* Value, of 3 Years old, at 2 *l.* 10 *s.* of 2 Years, at 2 *l.* of 1, at 1 *l.* An Ox of 4 Years, at 5 *l.* A Horfe, or Mare of 3 Years, at 5 *l.* of 2 Years, at 3 *l.* of 1, at 1 *l.* 10 *s.* A Sheep of 1 Year, at 10 *s.* A Goat, at 8. A Hog, at 20 *s.* An Afs, of 1 Year, at 2 *l.* Cattle under a Year, Corn and Hay in the Farmers Hands exempted.

Tradefmen and Artifans to be rated by Eftimation of their Profits, unlefs difabled.

Parents and Mafters fhall be tax'd for Children and Servants taking no Wages.

The Commiffioners to meet in the Shire-Town the firft *Wednefday* in *September*, to fign ther Lift and Affeffment, and give it to the Treafurer, or be fin'd 40 *s.* who is to levy it by the Conftables before the 20th of *November* every Year.

Every

Every Perſon is to pay the Conſtable where he is aſſeſs'd, who is to remit the Money to *Boſton*, if the Treaſurer deſires it, at the publick Expence.

Eſtates not laid to any Town to be aſſeſs'd in the neareſt.

Cows ſhall be taken in Payment, if no Price be ſet by the General Court, at a Price currant, judg'd by the Commiſſioners of *Eſſex*, *Middleſex*, and *Suffolk*.

Conſtables charg'd with Collections, ſhall clear Accounts before the firſt of *May*, on Penalty of 5 *l*.

The Treaſurer ſhall diſtrain on the Conſtables for Non-Payment, or anſwer it himſelf to the County : If nothing is to be found on the Conſtable, he may diſtrain on any able Man in the Town, who upon Petition, ſhall have Warrant to collect the Rates over again, with reaſonable Damages.

Conſtables charged with collections, may continue to finiſh their collections, and deſtrain for Non-Payment, after their Office is expired.

A Foreigner arriving with Goods to ſell, the ſelect Men may aſſeſs them according to Value, and iſſue a Warrant for levying it.

Miniſters are excus'd from all Taxes.

Children. All Parents to teach their Children to read, and all Maſters to acquaint their Families with the capital Laws, on Penalty of 20 *s*. and to catechiſe them once a Week.

The ſelect Men may examine Children and Apprentices, and admoniſh Parents and Maſters, if they find them ignorant, and with the conſent of two Magiſtrates, or the next County-Court, put them into better Hands.

Children ſo removed by the Magiſtrate, ſhall ſerve the Maſters they are plac'd with, Males 'till 21, Females 'till 18 Years of Age.

'Tis Death for any Child, above 16 Years of Age, and of ſound Underſtanding, to ſtrike, or curſe his Parent, unleſs provok d by extreme correction, or in their own Defence.

A Son of 16, accus'd by Parents of Rebellion, and other notorious crimes, ſhall be put to Death.

Magiſtrates may puniſh diſorderly Children or Servants on complaint, by Whipping, or otherwiſe, as they ſee

ſee cauſe, and bind them over to the next County-Court.

Whoever entices away, or entertains Children or Servants, to pay 40*s.*

Whoever gives credit, or lends Money to any under 21, ſhall loſe his Money, and anſwer for the Miſchief his doing ſo occaſion'd.

Children to be redreſt by the Magiſtrate, if deny'd convenient Marriage.

No Orphan to be diſpos'd of without conſent of ſome Court, the Majority of ſelect Men aſſenting, ſufficient in caſe of Marriage.

Women Minors 'till 16.

Chirurgeons and Midwives. No Surgeon, Midwife, or Phyſician, ſhall practiſe on any, without conſent of the Perſon, or neareſt Relation.

Civil Causes petty. Any Magiſtrate may ſummon, by the Conſtable, Parties and Witneſſes, and determine any cauſe without a Jury, Damages not exceeding 40*s.*

The County-Court may appoint three Inhabitants to determine them, where no Magiſtrate dwells, who muſt ſwear to be faithful, but may not commit to Priſon in any caſe.

If the Cauſe concerns the Magiſtrate, or any one of the Commiſſioners, the ſelect Men ſhall determine it.

Theſe little Cauſes ſhall not lye before the County Court, but by Appeal, unleſs in caſe of Aſſault, or Defamation.

The Freemen of *Boſton* may preſent ſeven to be ſworn by the Court of Aſſiſtants, as Commiſſioners for that Town, any three of which with a Magiſtrate, or five without, may determine any Civil cauſes under 10*l*, ariſing within the *Iſthmus*, or *Nottles-Iſland*, or in which either Party ſhall be an Inhabitant.

The Commiſſioners of *Boſton* ſhall keep Records, and publiſh their Court-Days; they may appoint their Clerks, and demand of the Plaintiff, in Actions under 40*s.* 3*s.* 6*d.* for others, 10*s.* and accuſtomed Fees.

They may take cognizance of Riots and criminal Miſdemeanors, not fining more than 40*s.*

They are to have their Commiſſions under the Hand of the Secretary of the General Court, and all Conſtables and Inhabitants are to aſſiſt them.

None

None to be admitted into this Office that are not faithful to their Country, and inoffenſive in their converſations; an Appeal lyes from them to the Court of Aſſiſtants.

Clerks. Clerks of the Writs are to be nominated by every Town, and and allow'd by the County Court.

They are to grant Summons, Attachments, and Replevies, and to take Securities for Proſecution of Suits.

Their Fees are, 2 *d.* for a Warrant, 3 *d.* for an Attachment Replevin, 4 *d.* for a Bond for themſelves; and 3 *d.* for the Mareſchal-General for Attachments.

Condemned Perſons. None to be executed 'till 4 Days after condemnation, but in caſe of martial Law, or ſome ſpecial cauſe, nor to remain unburied 12 Hours, but in caſe of Anatomy.

The Dead Warrant to be ſign'd by the Secretary of the General Court.

Conſpiracy. Conſpiracy againſt the Commonwealth, by attempting an Invaſion, Inſurrection, Rebellion, or by attempting to ſeize any Towns or Forts, to be puniſh'd with Death.

Conſtables. Conſtables ſhall execute the Sentence on Criminals, or get one to do it.

They are to collect Rates, and Aſſeſſments, convey Offenders they are charg'd with before ſome Magiſtrate, receive and forward all Hue and Cries after Offenders, and even iſſue them when no Magiſtrate is near.

He may ſearch for Offenders in publick Houſes, and apprehend them without Warrant; but if employ'd, he muſt have a Warrant.

Whoever refuſes to aſſiſt the Conſtable, muſt pay 10 *s.* to the Country, to be levy'd by Warrant, if he does it contemptuouſly, he muſt pay 40 *s.*

Every Conſtable muſt have a black Staff 5 Foot long, tipt at the upper End 5 Inches with Braſs, as the Badge of his Office, when he acts.

If the Conſtable refuſes to forward a Hue and Cry; he ſhall pay 40 *s.*

The Conſtables may arreſt, and ſerve Summons and Attachments, where no Marſhal lives.

The Charge of Hue and Cry after a Priſoner muſt be

be paid by the Treaſurer of the County; after others, by thoſe who procure them.

Conveyances. No Alienation of Lands, but by Deed ſign'd and deliver'd, and Poſſeſſion given by the Seller, or one authoriz'd by him. The clauſe of Conveyance to be in theſe Words: *To have and to hold the ſaid Premiſes reſpectively to the Party, or Grantee, his Heirs and Aſſigns for ever:* If the Eſtate be entail'd, in theſe Words: *To have, and to hold,* &c. *to the Party or Grantee, and to the Heirs of his Body lawfully begotten between him, and ſuch a one his Wife.* This Form not neceſſary in granting Town-Lands.

Former Deeds remain good, though not in the Methods now preſcribed.

Deeds obtain'd by Violence are void, fraudulent Conveyances ſhan't defeat a Man of his Claim to juſt Debts, Licences, or Lands.

No Grants, Sales, or Mortgages ſhall be in Force, except againſt the Grantee, himſelf, or Heirs, unleſs own'd before a Magiſtrate, and recorded.

All Grants before *October* 1640, to be recorded, in a Month, or to be null, except againſt the Grantee; if he refuſes to own the Grant, when requir'd, the Magiſtrate may commit him, and the Grantee enter a Caution with the Recorder of the County-Court, which ſhall ſecure his Intereſt.

The Clerk of the County-Court to enter all Grants, Sales, *&c.* with the Names of Granter and Grantee, with the Date, and Particulars of the Eſtate.

If the Granter be not in the Juriſdiction, he muſt enter within three Months after his Return.

General Court. The General Court made up of Magiſtrates and Deputies, hath Power to tax the Country, and to give, and confirm Properties of publick Lands. It hath the Supreme Legiſlative Power, and the Power of Judicature, and of redreſſing the Grievances of the People; the Deputies muſt take the following Oath.

I Do ſwear by the moſt great and dreadful Name of the ever-living God, that in all Caſes wherein I am to deliver my Vote or Sentence againſt any criminal Offence, or between Parties in any Civil Caſe, I will deal uprightly and

and justly, according to my Judgment and Conscience, and I will according to my Skill and Ability, assist in all other publick Affairs of this Court faithfully and truly, according to the Duty of my Place, when I shall be present to attend the Service.

The Magistrates and Deputies in this Court must sit and act apart, and Laws and Orders must be transmitted from one House to another; not to be in Force 'till passed by a Majority in both Houses, and engrossed.

They are to be read the last Day of the Session to the whole Body united.

In case of Difference, 'tis to be decided by the Majority of both Houses met together.

This Court to be call'd by Governour, Deputy-Governour, or Court of Assistants on any Occasion, but to be dissolv'd, or adjourn'd only by themselves.

It assembles by Warrant once a Quarter, or oftner.

It may call the Governour or any Magistrate to Account, and censure them, as the case requires.

It may determine causes without Appeal, and cite those depending in other Courts.

The Governour to have the casting Vote in this, as the Moderator in other Civil Assemblies.

County Court. The County Court consists of Magistrates of the County, and others appointed by the General Court at the Nomination of the Freemen, five of them with one Magistrate may hold a Court.

They may determine causes not extending to Life, Member, or Banishment, appoint Clerks, and other Officers, and summon Juries for the several Townships.

Courts of Assistants. Courts of Assistants consist of Governour, Deputy-Governour, and Magistrates of *Boston*, who are to meet at *Boston* the first *Tuesday* in *March* and *September*.

They determine Actions of Appeal, capital causes, and causes of Divorce: They may be called by the Governour, or his Deputy, as Occasion requires: Seven must be present, of which the Governour, or his Deputy, to be one, except in cases of necessity.

Courts Special. The Governour or Deputy, with two Magistrates, or any three Magistrates may call a special Court for the sake of a Stranger.

The

The Records of it to be enter'd in the Court of Affiftance, at the Expence of the Party caft.

Courts in General. Any Court may receive an Action from a Stranger, againft any one not an Inhabitant, and proceed to Judgment on Proof of legal Summons.

All criminal Cafes to be try'd at the next Court that hath cognizance of them.

No Court is to transfer a Cafe to another, but they may ftate the Cafe and prefent it to the General Court for their Opinion, and proeecd to Judgment according to that Opinion.

Every Court may admit Freemen, if Church Members, and give them their Oath, and the Clerk muft fend their Names to the General Court.

Any one Magiftrate may adjourn the Court, and all Parties concern'd are bound without frefh Summons to attend again.

Clerks and Recorders of Courts muft be fworn to be faithful.

Cruelty. No Court can punifh with above Forty Stripes.

No Man muft correct any under him with Cruelty, or be cruel to a Beaft.

D.

Debts. No Debt not acknowledged for fix Years pleadable in any Court, unlefs prov'd or recorded in fome Court; the Evidence of fuch muft be fuch as the Court approves, the Debtor to have a Year to difprove it.

Deputies. The Deputies for the General Court are chofen by Ballots of Freemen.

They may confer about Bufinefs, and prepare it for the Court.

No Town can fend more than two; and a Town not having 20 Freemen, fends but one.

Freemen of a Plantation under 10, vote in the next Town.

They may chufe any one that is free, and lives within the Jurifdiction.

A

A Town not having 30 Freemen, may ſend Deputies, or let it alone.

Diſputes about Elections decided by the Deputies in the General Court.

No Man to be a Deputy, who is not ſound in the main Points of Religion, regular in his Converſation, or faithful to the Government; whoever Votes knowingly for ſuch, pays 5 *s*.

The Conſtable to return the Perſon choſen, and the Time for which, on forfeiture of 20 *s*.

They are not to be continued above a Year.

They muſt attend the Court, or pay 20 *s*. a Day, if not excus'd by the Houſe.

No Attorney in an Inferior Court to ſit in the General Court.

Diſtreſs. Things ſubject to preſent Decay, as Corn, *&c.* not liable to Diſtreſs, unleſs Security be given to make good the Damages.

Dowry. Wives not endowed by Jointure before Marriage, have a Right to a Third of the Husband's Eſtate for their Life, unleſs barr'd from it by her Conſent in Writing, own'd before a Magiſtrate.

The Heir at Law is to aſſign her Thirds within a Month, or ſhe may bring a Writ of Dowry in the County Court.

They muſt leave the Eſtate aſſign'd them, in repair.

E.

Elections. Aſſiſtants are choſen by Freemen putting a Bean againſt the Perſon, or a Grain of Corn for him.

Whoever puts in one or more Beans that is not Free, pays 10 *s*.

Any one may ſeal up his Vote before the Conſtable or Deputy, and ſend it to the Court of Elections at *Boſton*.

The Governour, his Deputy, Major-General, Treaſurer, Secretary, and Commiſſioners of the United Colonies are elected by Papers ſent open with their Names.

Magiſtrates for Towns are to be choſen by Freemen ſummoned in the ſecond Week of *March*.

He

He that gives more than one Vote in any Election, to pay 10*s*.

The Votes for the Aſſiſtants are to be ſent from each Town to the Shire-Town, and thence to *Boſton* to be open'd before a Magiſtrate the ſecond *Tueſday* in *April*; and the 18 that have moſt Voices, are to be Magiſtrates and Aſſiſtants.

The Commiſſioner who brought the Votes, to return the Names of thoſe choſen to the Conſtables, and they to the Freemen.

Whoever performs not his Duty in Elections, pays 10*s*.

No Quaker or Diſſenter from the Publick Worſhip has a Vote.

Eſcheates. Where there is no Heir, the Eſtate is to be in the Treaſury till a legal Claim be made.

F.

Falſe-Witneſſing. 'Tis Death to attempt another's Life by witneſſing falſely, wittingly and willingly.

Farms. Farms within the Bounds of a Town, are part of that Town, *Meadford* excepted.

Fees. Whoever impleads another, in County-Court, or Court of Aſſiſtants, pays 10 *s*. before the *Cauſe* be entered.

Ten Shillings muſt be paid for every Action before the Commiſſioners of *Boſton* that's above 40*s*. 3 *d*. and 4 *d*. for one under it, either before them or any Magiſtrate, or the three Commiſſioners for ſmall Cauſes.

The Court may excuſe Fees.

Fifteen Shillings muſt be paid, where Damages are recovered above 10 *l*. 20 *s*. where 20 *l*.

All Fees to be allow'd in the Judgment levy'd by the Marſhal, and accounted to the reſpective Treaſurer.

Fences. Every one to fence according to his Proportion of the Corn-field in common, and not to put in Cattle while any Corn remains.

If they can't agree, ſelect Men to determine, or the Freemen where there are none.

Whoever won't ſtand to their Determination muſt incloſe his own Part.

Select

Select Men may order the Fences within their Bounds in Farms under 100 Acres, and impose Fines on Defaulters under 20 *s.*

If they neglect the Fences, to pay 5 *s.* to the Town *per* Month.

They may appoint two or more yearly to view the the Fences, and give Notice to the Owners to repair them, and if they do it not in six Days, the Surveyor may do it, and recover double Wages, to be levy'd by the Constable, having a Warrant from the select Men.

If any one fences his Lands, his Neighbour is not to pay half of the Charge till he also incloses.

The first Incloser is not to lay open his Neighbour's Land, tho' he may his own, but may demand the Value of half the Party-fence to be set by two, each chusing one, and purchase it.

This holds good in case of a Town-Common, but not of House Lots, under 10 Acres; if such are improv'd, the Neighbour pays half the Party-Fence, whether he improves or not.

If a Person receives Damage from Cattle because his Fence was faulty, he cannot recover it.

Ferries. No Passenger to be transported but by authoriz'd Ferry-men, who can only take up at their own Ferry Place, tho' they may land at anothers.

No Canoe to be us'd by them, on Forfeiture of the Canoe or Value of it, unless in case of Necessity.

Persons may pass in their own or Neighbours Boats.

Passage at *Weymouth-Ferry* 2 *d.* after Day-light is over 4 *d.*

Magistrates and Deputies pass free with a Servant and Horse, except where Rent is paid to the Country.

Whoever presses into a Ferry-boat, without consent of Ferryman or Passengers, he may be thrust out, or pays 10 *s.*

If the Ferryman admits one against the Consent of any Magistrate, Deputy or Elder, or Majority of the Passengers, he pays 20 *s.*

Persons to be transported in their Turn, except Publick Officers, Physicians, and such-like, who are to be taken first.

Fines. Persons are to stay in Prison till they pay their Fines, unless the Judge or Court respite them.

The

The Clerk of the Court is to give a Copy of Fines and Dues to the Treaſurer, who muſt iſſue his Warrant to the Mareſchal to levy them.

The ſelect Men are to receive Fines in caſe of Elections for the uſe of the poor.

Firing. Whoever kindles a Fire in a Wood, ſo as to hurt Corn, before the 20th of *April*, or on *Saturdays* or *Sundays*, pays the Damage, and half ſo much to the Country.

If not able to pay, is to be whipt with Twenty Stripes.

Whoever ſets fire to any thing, to pay double Damage and be whipt, if Ten Years old.

If it be a Houſe or ſuch-like, 'tis Death, with the Forfeiture of what makes Satisfaction.

Perſons ſuſpected of this, to be impriſoned without Bail till the next County Court.

Fiſh. Fiſhermen may uſe Harbour or adjoyning Land for curing their Fiſh, and take what Timber or Fire wood they want, paying the Proprietor.

A Surveyor of Fiſh muſt be choſen by Buyer and Seller; what he ſays is merchantable, the Buyer muſt take, he muſt be ſworn before one appointed to take his Oath by the General Court; he is to have a Penny *per* Quintal, to be paid, half by the Buyer, and half by the Seller.

All Fiſh ſalted with *Sucktood*, Sun burnt, Salt burnt dry Fiſh, Fiſh pickled, is unmerchantable.

No one to kill Cod-fiſh, Hake, Haddock or Polluck for ſale in *December* or *January*, or Mackarel to barrel in *May* or *June*, on the Penalty of 5 *s.* for every Quintal, and the Mackarel forfeited.

The Garbage not to be thrown near the Banks.

Fiſhermen diſobeying Orders, or getting drunk, to pay for the firſt Offence 20 *s.* for the ſecond 40 *s.* and to be impriſoned three Months for the third.

Forgery. Forgery is puniſh'd with the Pillory, double Damages, and being diſabled to give Evidence or Verdict.

Fornication. Puniſh'd by compelling Marriage, Fines, or as the Court ſees fit.

Freemen. All *Engliſhmen*, Members of Churches found

found in Faith, regular in Life, Free-holders, rateable at 10 *s.* being 24 Years old, may be made free.

Not exempted from Offices, tho' they take not up their Freedom.

The County Court administers the Oath of a Freeman, to any admitted by the General Court.

Galloping Horses. No one to gallop a Horse in *Boston*, on Penalty of 3 *s.* 4 *d.*

Gaming. Whoever games for Money, pays treble the Value, half to the Treasurer, half to the Informer.

No playing at Shuffleboard or Bowls at a Publick House, on Penalty of 20 *s.* to the Master, and 5 to the Player.

No Dancing in Publick Houses, on Penalty of 5 *s.*

No Feasts or Festivals to be observ'd, or Cards or Dice to be us'd, on Penalty of 5 *s.*

None to bring Cards or Dice into the Country, or to have any in their custody, on Penalty of 5 *l.* half to the Treasurer, half to the Informer.

Whoever delivers them up is excus'd; whoever games, and informs of himself, is excus'd; he may witness against others, but has no Benefit from informing against them.

Judges may change the Fine into corporal Punishment.

H.

Heresy. Whoever denies the Immortality of the Soul, the Resurrection of the Body, or the Evil done by the outward Man is Sin, or that Christ gave himself a Ransom for Sins, or that we are justified by his Righteousness or the Morality of the 4th Command, or the baptizing of Infants, or the Ordinance of Magistracy, or their Authority to make War, or punish Offenders against the first Table; whoever denies any of these, or seduces others to do so, must be banish'd the Jurisdiction.

Whoever professing the *Christian Religion*, and being 16, denies any Book of the Bible to be the Word of God, is to be imprison'd till the County Court, and fin'd or punish'd, as the Court thinks fit.

If he recants before Sentence, not to be fin'd above 10 *l.*

If

If he offends afterwards, he is to die or be baniſh'd, as the Court thinks fit.

The blaſphemous Books of *Veers* or *Muggleton* to be deliver'd up to the Magiſtrate and burnt, on Penalty of 10 *l.*

Whoever knowingly brings a Quaker or Heretick, is impriſon'd till he pays or gives Security for 100 *l.* and carrying him away again.

Whoever conceals ſuch, to pay 40 *s.* an Hour, or lie in Priſon till he does.

Whoever goes to a Quaker's-Meeting, pays 10 *s.* and 5 *l.* if he preaches.

Whoever diſperſes or conceals their Books, pays 5 *l.* for every Book.

Whoever reviles Magiſtrates or Miniſters, pays 5 *l.* or is to be whipp'd.

Defamers of Magiſtrates or Judges, for what they do in Court, are to be puniſh'd as the Crime deſerves.

The Publiſher of any Error to be cenſur'd as he deſerves by the County Court.

Quakers not Inhabitants, to be impriſon'd till the Court of Aſſiſtants, and then baniſh'd; not to return on Pain of Death.

If Inhabitants, they are to give Security for appearing next General Court, and to be baniſh'd if they don't recant.

If he returns, to be baniſh'd again, not to return on Pain of Death.

Vagabond Quakers are whipt through the Towns, not exceeding three, and convey'd out of the Juriſdiction; if they return after three Times, they are to be in the Houſe of Correction till County Court, branded with the Letter *R* on the left Shoulder, and whipp'd, as before; if they return after this, to be baniſh'd on Pain of Death.

If any turn Quakers, they are to be baniſh'd the Juriſdiction, and ſerv'd as Vagabond Quakers, if they return.

The Magiſtrate ſigning the Warrant for Whipping, muſt mention the Towns and Number of Stripes, and the Conſtable ſee it executed at the Expence of the County.

Hides.

Hides. No raw Hides, Skins, *&c.* to be expoſed, except thoſe which have been imported, or the Skins of wild Beaſts, on Penalty of the Goods or Value.

Highways. Highways muſt be kept in Repair by the Publick.

New Roads are to be laid out by three Men of the next Towns appointed by the County Court, without pulling down Houſes, or laying open Gardens, and to be 10 Rods wide where the Ground is wet or rocky.

The Town pays the Damage done to improv'd Lands, as valu'd by thoſe who lay out the Road; thoſe aggriev'd may appeal to the County Court.

If it be without cauſe, they muſt pay Charges and a Fine.

The ſelect Men to lay out private Roads, ſo as no Damage be done, without any Recompence.

Gates or Rails in the Road may be pull'd up by the County Court, paying Damages to the Owners.

Horſes. No Horſe to be ſold to an *Indian*, on Penalty of a 100 *l.* or taken on Board a Veſſel, without being enter'd in the Toll-Book, with the Colour, Mark and Age of the Horſe, with the Name of the Perſon of whom bought, and Proof that he was the Owner of it, on Penalty of 4 *l.* half to the Informer.

No Stone-Horſe above two Years old to run at large, unleſs view'd and allow'd of by the ſelect Men, on Penalty of 20 *s.* *per* Month.

If they neglect to view the Horſe or levy the Fine, they pay 20 *s.*

I.

Jaylors. Jaylors may take Bail in Civil Caſes, after Commitment.

Idle Perſons. Idle Perſons are to be preſented and puniſh'd, as the Court ſees fit.

Jeſuits. No Jeſuit or Prieſt to abide in the Juriſdiction.

Whoever can't clear himſelf from Suſpicion to the Court of Aſſiſtants, to be baniſh'd, not to return on Pain of Death, unleſs by Shipwreck, or in Company with

with any upon Bufinefs, with whom they are to return.

Whatever Prieft refiding there, did not depart before *November* 1700, he was to be imprifon'd for Life, and to die if he broke Prifon.

Whoever conceal'd fuch, to be Pillory'd, or pay 200 *l.* half to the Informer.

Any Juftice may commit one fufpected, in order to a Trial, and he may be feiz'd by any, without Warrant.

If a Prieft is driven on the Coaft, he muft go to one of the Council, obferve his Orders and depart as foon as poffible.

Impofts. Wines and Strong Waters not coming from *England*, are to be enter'd, on Forfeiture of the Goods; the Duty of fuch Goods to be paid in kind, as the Owner can agree with the Officer.

The Cuftomer may employ Deputies to wait or fearch Wines.

Wines of *Fyal* or *Weftern Iflands*, pay 5 *s.* *per* Pipe; of *Madera* 6 *s.* 8 *d.* Sherry, Sack or Canary, Muskadel, Tent, Malmfey, *Alicant*, or others from the Streights, 10 *s.* *French* 5 *s.* Strong Waters 40 *s.*

Conftables muft affift Officers in fearching for conceal'd Wines, in order to feize them, on Forfeiture of 10 *s.*

Debts due for Cuftom, where Wines and Strong Waters are not to be had, are recoverable by Action.

Ships not fraught in *England*, pay 6 *d.* *per* Ton, and 10 *s.* *per* Ship to maintain Fortifications, thofe fraught in *England*, 10 *s.* *per* Ship, if above 100 Ton, if under, 6 *s.* 8 *d.* *per* Ton.

Publick Houfes to pay 2 *s.* 6 *d.* *per* Hogfhead for Syder, Ale and Beer, and 5 *s.* for Mum to the Treafurer, before whom he is to fwear to what he fells, or pay treble Duty, or lofe his Licenfe.

All imported Goods, except Fifh, Sheep, Wool, Cotton, Salt, pay 1 *d.* *per* Pound Value, to be rated at 20 *per Cent* above prime Coft.

The Mafter, before he breaks Bulk, muft report his Lading faithfully, on Penalty of 20 *s.* *per* Ton, and the Officer enter the Goods with the Owners Names, as far as they can lawfully be difcover'd, and the Owner fhall fhew his Invoyce, and difcover the Value of them to the Collector,

Collector, who muſt levy the Duty, and Diſtrain in caſe of Non-payment, taking 2 *s. per* Pound for his Labour.

If the Invoyce be ſatisfied, the Collector, with the ſelect Men rate the Goods.

Cattle brought into this Juriſdiction, to be ſold, kill'd or tranſported, to be paid for according to the Law mention'd, Tit. *Charges of the Publick*, on Forfeiture of the Beaſt or Value, half to the Informer.

Goods brought by Land, to pay 1 *d. per* Pound in Money, before Sale or Exportation.

The County Treaſurer is to ſee this Law executed.

No Goods paid for by this Law, are rateable again the ſame Year.

The Treaſurer may apply to the Council for Direction in doubtful Caſes.

Maſters of Ships bringing rateable Goods, muſt have Orders from the Treaſurer to deliver them, or pay the Rate ; the Seal of his Office is (*TM*).

Impreſs. One Magiſtrate and the Overſeer may Impreſs any Labourers for publick Work, authorized by the General Court for a Week, paying them Wages, unleſs they have ſome Incapacity.

A Perſon may be forc'd to go out of his Juriſdiction only in Caſe of a defenſive War, enter'd upon by the General Court.

No Man's Cattle or Goods to be Impreſs'd without Warrant, and paying reaſonable Prizes, and making good all Damage.

Impriſonment. No one to be Impriſon'd, but in ſuch Caſes as the Law allows of.

Indians. *Indians* have a Right to Lands ſubdu'd and improv'd, deſiring to live among the *Engliſh*.

They ſhall have Allotments of Lands, according to Cuſtom, and have Relief in Courts, if diſpoſſeſs'd of what is theirs, as the *Engliſh*.

Lands in the Juriſdiction not improv'd by *Indians*, is the Property of the *Engliſh*.

None to buy Land of *Indians*, without Leave from the General Court, on Forfeiture of the Lands.

None to ſell to the *Indians*, or to any Perſons inhabiting out of the Juriſdiction, Guns, Powder, Ball, Armour

or

or Weapon, on Forfeiture of 40 *s.* for a pound of Lead or Shot, 5 *l.* for every pound of Powder, and 10 *l.* for Gun, Armour or Weapon.

No Perſon not in the Juriſdiction may Trade with any *Indian* within this Juriſdiction for any Goods, without forfeiting them.

They may be ſeiz'd by any without Warrant, half for their own Uſe.

He that ſells any ſort of Peltry to the *Indians*, without Leave from the General Court, pays 100 *l.* 10 *l.* for the Informer.

Whoever ſells them any ſtrong Liquors, pays 40 *s.* a Pint; a Third to the Informer.

Trucking Houſes not allow'd by the General Court, are to be demoliſh'd.

Phyſicians may preſcribe in Liquors forbid to the *Indians*, with Licenſe of a Magiſtrate.

None to ſell the *Indians* a Boat, Skiff or Canoe, on Forfeiture of 50 *l.*

Damage done their Corn, to be recompenc'd by thoſe whoſe Cattle did it.

Thoſe whoſe Cattle may damage their Plantations, muſt help them to fence, and they muſt ſell them Tools to do it.

If they refuſe to fence, they can't have Damage.

They muſt fence Lands granted or purchaſed, at their own Charge.

If the *Indian* Cattle damage the *Engliſh*, they muſt make Satisfaction.

Laws reſpecting them, muſt be made known to them once a Year, by one appointed by the General Court.

Civiliz'd *Indians* living under the Government, ſhall have an *Indian* Commiſſioner, and Conſtables and Marſhals in their Plantations, and the Power of a County Court to determine Cauſes, provided an *Engliſh* Magiſtrate appoint the Time and Place, and conſents to all Judgments.

Indians not to profane the Sabbath, or to have ſtrong Liquors.

If Drunk, they muſt pay 10 *s.* or be whipp'd with Ten Stripes, confeſs where they had the Liquor, or ſtay in the Houſe of Correction, till they pay the Fine of the Liquor they drank.

The

The Accuſation of an *Indian* will be good againſt any that purgeth not himſelf by Oath.

Thoſe who have Licenſe to ſell Peltry to the *Indians*, may alſo ſell Arms and Ammunition to thoſe not in Hoſtility, paying to the Treaſurer every half Year 6 *s. per* pound of Powder: 6 *d.* for 10 pound of Shot: 3 *s. per* Gun and *per* dozen of Sword-Blades, and give a true account upon Oath of what he ſells, on Penalty of 5 *l.* for every pound of Powder; 5 *l.* for every 10 pound of Shot; 10 *l.* for every Gun or dozen of Sword-Blades; this to be in Force while the Court pleaſes. 1668.

Indictments. The Indictment muſt be within a Year after the Offence, except in capital Offences, Crimes that concern Life, or Member, or Baniſhment, Treaſon, Conſpiracy or Felony, above 10 *s.* or Civil Right or Cauſe of Action at Law.

Inn-keepers. None to keep a Publick Houſe without Licenſe from the County Court, on penalty of 5 *l.* or Impriſonment during Pleaſure.

Merchants not to Retail under three Gallons of Wine or Syder, and a Quart of Strong Waters.

Publick Houſes muſt have a Sign within three Months, or forfeit their Licenſe.

And ſell Beer at 2 *d. per* Quart, 4 Buſhels of Malt to the Hogſhead, on penalty of 40 *s.*

If they brew with any thing inſtead of Malt, to pay 5 *l.*

They muſt ſuffer none to be drunk, or to have above half a pint of Wine, or to ſit above half an Hour, or after Nine at Night, on penalty of 5 *s.*

If they conceal a Drunkard, or ſend not for the Conſtable, they pay 5 *l.*

Whoever is drunk, pays 3 *s.* 4 *d.* for drinking too much; 2 *s.* 6 *d.* for ſtaying more than half an Hour; and 5 *s.* for ſitting after Nine at Night; to be impriſon'd till he pays, or ſit in the Stocks 3 Hours.

If he abuſes the Conſtable, or ſtrives to Eſcape, he may commit him till he pays, or till Order from the Magiſtrate.

Licens'd Houſes may entertain Travellers or Seafaring Men in the Night.

Private Perſons pay 20 *s.* or ſit in the Stocks for the firſt Offence, in permitting People to tipple in their Houſes

Houſes ; 5 *s.* for the ſecond ; to be bound to better Behaviour or committed for the third.

Merchants of Wine to pay 10 *s.* if any drink to Exceſs in their Cellars.

Drunkards forfeit double for the ſecond Offence, and treble for the third ; if not able to pay it, they muſt be whipp'd with ten Stripes.

They muſt be committed for the fourth Offence, or find Sureties for their good Behaviour.

Perſons keeping a Publick Houſe, ſhall be diſabled from keeping one for ever, if they offend in this *Point* the third time.

Whatever Victualler is not provided to entertain Strangers Horſes with Stable Room and Attendance, pays 2 *s.* 6 *d.* and double Damages.

Retailers pay 5 *s. per* But of Wine, and 2 *d. per* Quart of Strong Waters to the Country ; the Duty to be accounted for, and an account of what the Retailer buys to be given every ſix Months to the Treaſurer, or the Wine is forfeited, half to the Treaſurer and Informer.

They muſt not ſell Wine above 6 *d.* a Quart more than what it coſt them *per* Butt.

The Treaſurer may appoint Officers to collect this Duty, and take it in Wines or other Goods ; he is to have 2 *s.* in the pound.

Whoever ſells Drink, except to a Stranger, in Time of a Lecture, pays 5 *s.*

Offences againſt this Law determin'd by one Magiſtrate, who may warrant the Conſtable to levy the Fines.

One Confeſſing, is good Witneſs againſt another.

Conſtables may ſearch for Offenders on Lord's-Days and Lecture-Days ; they forfeit 10 *s.* for any Neglect.

Licenſes muſt be renewed every Year, on penalty of 5 *l.*

This does not extend to Vintners under Contract with the Publick.

Perſons diſturbing the Houſe where they drink, pay 5 *s.* if the Maſter ſuffers it, his Licenſe ſhan't be renew'd.

Thoſe who are with them are Guilty, unleſs they teſtify their Diſlike.

Thoſe who are addicted to Tippling, and warn'd by ſelect

ſelect Men not to frequent Taverns, ſhall pay 5 *s.* if found in a publick Houſe.

Keepers of publick Houſes muſt have a Licence, not to entertain ſuch Perſons : if they do, to pay 20 *s.*

Judges. No Perſon is to ſit as Judge in a Cauſe when his Relation is concern'd.

Judgments. If a Judgment or Execution be ſold it is void in Law.

If the Party dyes before he has had Satisfaction, his Executor ſhall renew it.

Judgment confeſs'd before two Magiſtrates is good, the Clerk may receive a Shilling Fee.

If a Perſon whoſe Goods are taken in Execution owns what is not his own, he makes it good, and pays double Damages.

If other Perſon's Goods be ſeiz'd in Execution, they muſt be reſtor'd, and another Execution granted, as if no Goods had been ſeiz'd at all.

Juries. The Clerk in Court muſt ſend a Warrant to Conſtables to ſummon Jurymen, in proportion to the Inhabitants.

He muſt give Notice to the Freemen to chuſe and return thoſe choſen.

None muſt be warn'd from *Salem* to *Ipſwich*, or *Ipſwich* to *Salem*.

In ſpecial Courts Jurymen have 4 *s.* a Day from thoſe who deſir'd that Court.

The Juries at the Court of Aſſiſtants are choſen in *Suffolk* and *Middleſex*.

Jurors ſworn are to find the Fact according to Evidence, the Judge to determine Matter of Equity.

Caſes of Life or Baniſhment try'd in inferior Courts, only by ſpecial Jury.

Grand Juries ſummoned once a Year to preſent Miſdemeanors.

No Juror ſhall diſcover a Crime, when under Tye of Conſcience to the contrary, except the publick would ſuffer, or legal Teſtimony is requir'd.

Every Grand Juryman is to have 3 *s.* a Day out of the Perquiſites of the Court.

The Jury may bring in their Verdict ſpecial, and then the Court determines.

Ju-

Jurors may find in their Verdict as much as they can, if they can't find the main Issue.

If the Court and Jury differs, the case issues in the Court of Assistants.

They may there bring new Pleas and Evidence.

If the Plaintiff pursues not his Cause there, the Defendant is to have Costs the next County Court.

Any Juror not satisfy'd, may openly in Court consult with any Man.

No Juror is forc'd to serve above one ordinary Court in a Year, except summoned, in cases of Life, or Banishment.

Grand Juries must serve two Courts together at least.

Plaintiffs or Defendants not appearing, are nonsuited, and to pay Costs to him who does appear.

The Parties may agree to try it afterwards, the Plaintiff paying half Fees for a new Entry.

Any presented by the Grand Jury, or summon'd by the Magistrate, must be proceeded against for Contempt, if they don't appear.

In all Civil Cases the Verdict of the Jury must be accepted. But upon apparent corruption, the Party aggriev'd may attaint the Jury, and have Execution respited, upon his being bound to prosecute at the next Court of Assistants, and the Clerk summons a new Jury of 24, to try the Action of Attaint.

If they find for the Plaintiff, the former Defendant pays Damages, if corruption be found in the Jurors, the Court fines, or imprisons ; if they are acquitted, the Plaintiff pays double Damages, the former Judgment is good, and Execution issued.

L.

Lands. All Lands are Freeholds, and subject to no Fines upon Alienations, nor Harriots, Wardships, Escheats, or Forfeitures, on the Death of Parents, or Ancestors for ever.

Leather. None but Tanners are to tan, on Forfeiture of 6*s.* 8*d.*

Whoever cuts the Hide in fleaing, pays 1*s.* for every cut.

Lea-

Leather badly tann'd is forfeited, if expos'd to Sale.

Tanners having their Fatts in improper Places, or putting Leather in warm Moors, pay 20 *l.*

Curriers not to drefs Leather badly tann'd, but to curry Leather well, on Forfeiture of the Hide that is prejudic'd.

Every Town muft appoint Perfons to view the Leather, to feal what is good, and feize what is otherwife.

If the Owner fubmits not, it is to be view'd by four skilful Perfons, who are to make their Report to the next County Court.

The Officer's Fee for Sealing is 1 *d.* *per* Hide for Parcels under five, and 6 *d.* for every Dickar above.

If he is not faithful, he forfeits the Value of the Leather.

Fines are paid, a Third to the Shire, a Third to the Town, and a Third to the Seizer.

Liberties. Any Perfon may come into Court, or Council, and move for any thing in a decent Manner.

Every Houfholder has free Fifhing and Fowling, in any River, Bay, *&c.* within the Precincts of the Town where they dwell, fo far as the Sea ebbs and flows, unlefs it be appropriated by the Freemen.

No Town to appropriate to one Perfon above ten Acres.

Lands adjoining have the Property to Low-water mark, but no Proprietor to hinder the Paffage of Boats where the Sea ebbs and flows.

Any may pafs thro' another's Lands, not trefpaffing on Corn, or Meadow.

Any one may remove himfelf out of the Jurifdiction.

Lying. Whoever publifhes a Lye to the Prejudice of the publick, or any private Perfon, pays 10 *s.* or fits in the Stocks two Hours for the firft Offence, for the fecond, 20 *s.* or whipp'd ten Stripes, for the third, 40 *s.* or fifteen Stripes; every new Fault increafes 10 *s.* or five Stripes.

Fines to be levy'd, or Punifhment inflicted by the Marfhal.

The Offender may appeal to the County Court.

If without Caufe, he pays double Fine.

Perfons muft correct their Children or Servants under Age for this Fault before the Officers.

Malt.

M.

Malt. Malt muſt be in good Condition, on Penalty of 1 *s. per* Buſhel.

No Wheat, Barley, Biſcuit, Beef, Flower, to be imported, on Penalty of Confiſcation.

Marſhals and Conſtables may ſeize wherever they find it, and have a fourth Part.

Manſlaughter. If any one ſhall kill another in defending himſelf, or one who attempts to rob, or murder, or break into a Dwelling Houſe, he ſhall be blameleſs.

Manſtealing. Whoever ſteals a Perſon, is to be put to Death.

Marriages. Whoever ſtrikes his Wife, or her Husband, is fin'd not exceeding 10 *l*, or otherwiſe puniſh'd, as the Court directs.

None are to be marry'd 'till it has been publiſh'd in the Meeting, where they dwell three Times, or affix'd to the Meetinghouſe Doors for 14 Days.

None are to court a Maid, without Conſent of her Parents, 5 *l.* for the firſt Offence, 10 *l.* for the ſecond, Impriſonment for the third, 'till releas'd by the County Court.

Marry'd Perſons muſt live together, unleſs the Court of Aſſiſtants approve of the Cauſe to the contrary.

None are to marry Perſons but the Magiſtrate.

None may marry the Siſter of a former Wife.

Marſhals. Every Court ſhall have a Marſhal to execute Writs, Summons, *&c.* and to levy Goods by Warrant, which he is to deliver to the Plaintiff, or make him Satisfaction.

Executions muſt be return'd to the Clerk that granted them, with an Account, and if the Plaintiff is not ſatisfy'd, the Clerk may grant Execution for what remains.

The Marſhal is to ſerve and return Attachments, to levy Fines by Warrant, or to pay 2 *s. per* Pound for what is not collected or return'd.

He is to be no Clerk nor Recorder.

His

His Fees are for Fines, 1 *s. per* Pound, for Attachments within a Mile 1 *s.* 3 *d.* for Executions 1 *s. per* Pound, for Sums under 10 *l*; 6 *d. per* Pound more, for all under 40 *l*; 3 *d.* more, for all under 100 *l*; 1 *d.* more, for all above, out of the Eſtate of the Defendant.

If his Fees anſwer not his travelling Charges, he has 6 *d. per* Mile.

He is to pay to the Marſhal-General 3 *d.* in 15 *d.* of Attachments, and 3 *d.* in 12 *d.* of Executions, who is alſo to have 2 *d. per* Quart of ſtrong Waters retail'd, the Benefit of importing them, and 50 *s.* of thoſe who ſell them without Licenſe, if he informs.

The Marſhal in levying Fines, *&c.* may after demand, break Doors, Locks, *&c.* and require Aſſiſtance.

He may levy Fines for whatever extraordinary Charges he is at.

He muſt not ſeize Bedding, Apparel, Tools, Arms, or what's neceſſary to Life.

No Officer is oblig'd to ſearch for any Man's Eſtate, but at the Place of Abode, he may take the Perſon, if he will not direct him to his Goods.

If he does any one an Injury, he may be ſu'd.

Maſters, Servants. Servants can't ſell any thing without Licence.

Workmen muſt work the whole Day; Time to be allow'd for Food and Reſt; the Freemen may ſettle the Rates of Labour and Time, and Men muſt work according to ſuch Rules.

If any Difference ariſe about it between Towns, the County Court decides it.

Servants running away may be brought back again by Force.

Wages may be paid in Corn, valued by two Freemen choſen; if theſe don't agree, the Magiſtrate or Conſtable chuſes a Third, who decides it.

Whoever flies from a cruel Maſter to a Freeman, may be harbour'd, giving Notice to the Maſter and Magiſtrate.

None are to be turn'd over for above a Year, but by Conſent of ſome Court.

If a Servant is hurt he goes free, and the Maſter recompences as the Court determines.

Faith-

Faithful Servants not to be ſent away empty, unfaithful not unpuniſh'd.

Militia. The Militia is commanded by a Major-General, that of *Suffolk*, *Middleſex* and *Eſſex* by the Serjeant-Major of each, that of *Norfolk* by the Major of *Eſſex*.

The Serjeant-majors are choſen by the Freemen and Houſholders, by a Warrant from the Major-General.

They muſt exerciſe their Regiments once in three Years, and have 20 *l.* for it out of the Treaſury.

They may fine and levy upon Delinquents, with Conſent of their Officers.

Houſholders and Freemen choſe the Officers, to be confirm'd by the County Court.

Towns chargeable with 64 Soldiers ſhall chuſe all Officers, and form a Company, others only Serjeants and Corporals, the Major joyning ſmall Towns into a Company.

Officers muſt have their Commiſſion from the General Court, and take Care of the Equipage of their Companies, and exerciſe them ſix Times a Year, and puniſh Diſorders corporally, or by Fine, under 20 *s.*

Soldiers and all Inhabitants are to be furniſh'd with Arms, on Penalty of 20 *s.* and Males above ſixteen to attend Exerciſes, on Penalty of 5 *s.* except Magiſtrates, Deputies, Officers of Court, Elders and Deacons, thoſe of *Harvard*-College, School-maſters, Phyſicians and Surgeons, Treaſurers, Surveyors-General, publick Notary, Maſters of Ships above 20 Ton, Fiſhermen at fiſhing Seaſons, conſtant Herdſmen, one Servant of a Magiſtrate and teaching Elder, the Sons and Servants of the Major-General, and thoſe who are infirm.

The Clerk of every Company muſt keep a Liſt, take Notice of Offenders, view Arms and Ammunition twice a Year, and give an Account to the Captains, and levy Fines, and lay them out for Trophies, Colours, Drums, Halberds, or Arms and Ammunition for the poorer Sort.

A Committee ſhall have Power in every Town to appoint a Watch.

The Committee of *Boſton*, *Charles-Town*, *Salem* and *Ipſwich* conſiſts of the chief Officer of Horſe, and a chief Officer of every Company of Foot.

Every

Every Committee is requir'd to give Notice of every Alarm to the Magiſtrate and Major.

On the Major's Death, the oldeſt Captain ſucceeds till Orders from the Superior.

Commiſſions take their Seniority from that of the Town they ſerve for, except thoſe of *Boſton*, who have their Seniority from the Date of their Commiſſions.

Commiſſioners of Militia alone, are to Impreſs Soldiers, and take care of Fortifications and Artillery.

Watches are ſet half an Hour after Sun-ſet; and none to fire a Gun afterwards, on penalty of 40 *s*.

They may detain any they ſuſpect till Morning.

If any reſiſt a Centinel in time of War, he may fire on him, and give the Alarm.

Smiths are to repair Arms brought to them immediately, in Time of War; and within 10 Days in Time of Peace, on penalty of 10 *s*.

Every Town muſt have a Magazine, on penalty of 10 *s*.

The ſelect Men muſt provide a Quintal of Powder, a Quintal and half of Musket-Ball, and 28 pound of Match to every 50 Men, and renew it, on penalty of five pound.

The Horſe are commanded by the Majors of the Counties, and every Company chuſe their Officers.

Every Trooper is to have a good Horſe, with Furniture, on penalty of 10 *s*. and not to change it, or diſband himſelf without Leave, under penalty of a Fine not exceeding 50 *s*. at the Diſcretion of the Officer.

He muſt attend ſix Days Exerciſe every Year, or pay 5 *s*. on every Default.

The Clerk of the Troop has the ſame Employment with him of a Company, only he is to have Marſhal's Fees for Travelling, and to levy no Fines within a Month after default.

In caſe of Alarm, all muſt repair to the Guard, or pay 5 pound.

None ſhall be liſted a Trooper, that is not rated 100 *l* in a ſingle Rate, or his Children.

Diſobedience of Orders puniſh'd as uſual, at the Diſcretion of the Officer.

All Perſons liable to ſerve in Conſtable's Watches, are ſo in Military.

Officers

Officers to obey the Major General.

All lifted in the Militia or extraordinary Troops, are fubject to *Marfhal Laws.*

Majors or Officers may march out of their County to annoy the Enemy; tho' not elfe; the chief Officer of a Place to be defended, is to command thofe pofted in it, unlefs the Major is prefent, or the General Court or Council order it otherwife.

The Commiffioners of War are not to pafs a Debenture of the Time a Man has ferv'd, without a Note of the Committee whence he came, certifying whether the Arms were his own, or are return'd.

If a Man is flain, the Certificate of a Captain will do.

The Committees may fortify their Towns, and appoint Garrifons, and oblige the Inhabitants to work, on penalty of 5 *s. per* Day.

They may difpofe of or augment their Magazines, and affefs the Town for it.

Fines not levy'd within a Month by the Clerk may be levy'd by the Marfhal on the Clerk himfelf for the Captain.

The Clerk is to account for all Fines with the Captain in fix Weeks.

Millers. Millers muft weigh all Corn, and take a 16th part for grinding.

Mines. Whoever difcovers a Mine in this Jurifdiction, enjoys the Profits thereof, with a fit Proportion of 21 Years; he may buy the Intereft of *Indians* in the Land where 'tis, but not enter on another's Property.

If he difcovers it in his own Land, 'tis his own for ever, except a fifth of the Oar.

Minifters. Every Town muft chufe a Minifter, and pay him according to Agreement; if not the Juftices may rate them according to their Ability.

If they are without one fix Months, the Quarter-Seffion gives them three Months to fupply themfelves.

If they ftill neglect it, they chufe for them, and oblige them to pay him.

Every Town having 50 Houfe-holders, fhall provide a School-mafter to teach to write and read; if it have 100, it fhall have a Grammar-School, the felect Men to fee them paid; whatever Town neglects it, pays 10 *l.*

Every

Every gather'd Church ſhall chuſe its Miniſter, and if the major part of the Inhabitants concur with the Church's Act, he ſhall be maintain'd by the Town.

The Town of *Boſton* was left by this Act to their own Cuſtoms.

Where no Church is gather'd, the rateable Inhabitants chuſe, with the Advice of three neighbouring Miniſters, giving 15 Day Notice.

If any refuſe to pay his proportion, he is fin'd by the Quarter-Seſſion, 40 *s.* for the firſt Offence, and 4 *l.* for every other.

If the Majority of the Inhabitants refuſe a Miniſter choſen by the Church, the Elders and Meſſengers of three or five Neighbouring Churches are call'd; if they approve of him, he is the Miniſter of the Town, and muſt be maintain'd.

Thoſe who voted as Church-members, may alſo vote as Inhabitants.

A Town neglecting a School, pays 20 *s.* every Maſter muſt be approv'd by the Miniſter, or two neighbouring Miniſters.

No Miniſter is to be a School-maſter.

The Quarter-Seſſions may appoint Men to aſſeſs and raiſe what is due to the Miniſter by Contract or Allowance ſettled by them, the Inhabitants to name the Aſſeſſor.

But if they won't act, the ſelect Men muſt.

Money. No Coin to be current, except *Engliſh*, or coin'd here of Silver of the Alloy of *Engliſh* Money, 2 *d. per* Shilling leſs Value than *Engliſh* Money.

Officers of the Mint are to have One Shilling in Twenty, every Shilling to weigh 3 Drams *Troy Weight*; other Pieces in the ſame proportion.

No one to carry more than 20 *s.* out of the Country, on penalty of the whole of his Eſtate, a Third to the Informer.

Monopolies. No Monopolies but of profitable Inventions, and for a ſhort Time.

Murder. Wilful Murder is puniſh'd with Death.

Oaths.

O.

Oaths, Subſcriptions. No Oaths or Subſcriptions are to be impos'd, but thoſe appointed by the General Court.

The County Court, or any Magiſtrate out of Cavit, is authoriz'd to require an Oath of Fidelity of all Inhabitants who have not taken it, and of Strangers after two Months Abode; if they refuſe, they forfeit 5 *s.* for every Week, or muſt give Security for their Fidelity.

P.

Payments. All Contracts muſt be paid in the Specie bargain'd for.

Petitions. All Petitions to the General Court, on common Occaſions, pay 2 *s.* 6 *d.* to the Clerk on Delivery.

Petitions for Abatement of Fines, Mitigation of Penalty, Gratuities, Debts, Controverſies, 10 *s.*

Petitions of Magiſtrates or Deputies either for themſelves or the Country exempted. The Clerks diſcount what is paid to them for Petitions in their Salary.

None are to be preſented to the General Court, after four Days of the Court of Elections, or the firſt Week of other Seſſions.

Pipe-ſtaves. The ſelect Men are to view Pipe-ſtaves before ſhipp'd, and to throw by thoſe that are any way defective, and to have 2 *s. per* Thouſand.

Thoſe offer'd to be ſhipp'd unſearch'd, are forfeited.

Maſters taking ſuch on Board, pay 5 *l.*

Refuſe-ſtaves may be ſold or ſhipp'd, if as ſuch, and not as merchantable.

Poor. The County Court, or two Magiſtrates, determine about Proviſion for the *Poor*, with an Appeal to the Court of Aſſiſtants.

Three Months Reſidence is a Settlement, except the ſelect Men warn them away, and complain to the County Court, if they ſtay.

Porters. The ſelect Men appoint *Porters*, and adjuſt their Wages.

Poſſeſſion. Poſſeſſion for five Years gives a Property.

Pound Breach. Every Village or Town muſt maintain a Pound.

Whoever impounds a Beaſt, muſt give Notice to the Owner, or cry them at the two next Markets or Lectures, and the Owner muſt pay Damages, tho' the Cattle eſcape.

Reſcuing Cattle going to pound, is fin'd 40 *s.* breaking the pound 5 *s.* to anſwer all Harm done, and to be whipp'd, if not able to make Satisfaction

Powder. The Captain of the Caſtle is to notify to all Maſters coming into the Bay, and the Conſtables to thoſe coming into other Ports, that they are to give an account of the Ammunition they bring to the Notary within a Month, with the Names of the Perſons to whom it is conſign'd, on penalty of 5 *l.*

No Gun-powder to be exported, without Licenſe, on penalty of Forfeiture.

The County Court may appoint Searchers to prevent it.

The Undertakers of the Powder-mill may have a Warrant to impreſs Men for publick Work.

Priſons. Malefactors are to be convey'd to *Priſon* at their own Charge, if they are able to bear it.

The County Court is to appoint a Houſe of Correction in every County, and a Maſter for it.

The ſelect Men are to provide Materials for Work, the Profit is the Maſter's, he allowing to the Offenders mean Food, or half what they earn.

Every one muſt be whipp'd at his Entrance, under 10 Stripes, and then employ'd by Task till diſcharg'd.

If they won't work, the Maſter muſt correct and abridge them of Food, and not diſcharge them without Warrant.

Whoever helps a Priſoner to eſcape, ſhall anſwer for him ; and ſuffer beſides, as the Court determines.

The Goaler is to ſuffer what the Priſoner deſerv'd, if he eſcapes thro' his Neglect.

Goalers

Goalers muſt give to the Courts from time to time true Liſts of their Priſoners.

The Courts determine what they are to be paid for their Maintenance, and by whom.

The Plaintiff in Civil Cauſes muſt give Security for Food and Phyſick, or the Priſoner ſwearing he is not worth 5 *l.* may be diſmiſs'd.

The ordinary Allowance is 2 *s.* 6 *d.* *per* Week for each Priſoner.

Proteſtation. Whoever diſſents from the Majority of the Court, may have his Proteſt enter'd, but without Reaſons.

Puniſhment. None to be twice puniſh'd for one Offence.

Corporal Puniſhments not to be Inhumane.

None to be whipp'd who can pay Fines, except the Caſe is extraordinary, and his Life ſcandalous.

None to be rack'd, unleſs it appears there are Confederates, and he won't diſcover them.

R.

Rape. Rapes are puniſh'd with Death, or ſome grievous Puniſhment the Court appoints inſtead of it.

Whoever has Carnal Knowledge of a Child under 10 Years of Age, ſuffers Death.

Records. All Judgments are to be recorded, and Evidences kept.

The Jury muſt deliver up the Writings committed to them when they give their Verdict.

Clerks of the Writs in every Town muſt record Births and Burials, and return a Copy to the Recorder of the County Court, paying a Penny for every Birth or Burial.

All Parents, or Maſters, or Executors, muſt notify to the Clerk every Birth or Death, and pay 3 *d.*

Every married Man ſhall notify to him his Marriage, under the Hand of the Magiſtrate who married him, and be enter'd paying 3 *d.* this alſo to be return'd as the other; Perſons not doing this, pay 1 *s.*

Clerks

Clerks not making their Annual return, pay 5 *l.* and 5 *s.* for omitting any particular Perſon.

Any Man may record Teſtimonies before two Magiſtrates, Deeds, or Evidence legally confirmed.

Any one may ſearch Records,or have Exemplifications.

Whoever defaces Records, pays treble Damages, and ſuffers otherwiſe, as the Court thinks fit.

Replevin. Perſons may replevy their Goods, except upon Execution or Fine, giving Security to proſecute the Replevin, and anſwer what ſhall be recover'd at Law.

S.

Sabbath. Whoever profanes the Sabbath after Admonition, pays for the firſt Offence 5 *s.* for the ſecond 10 *s.* to be bound over to the County Court for the third ; Governours of Youth under ſeven Years to ſuffer for them.

Drinking or ſporting on Saturdays after Su n pays 5 *s.* Perſons refuſing to pay, muſt ſuffer Corporal Puniſhment, as the Court determines.

No Work to be done on the Sabbath, on Penalty of 10 *s.* for the firſt Offence, to be doubled for every following one.

To travel to a Meeting not allow'd by Law, is a Profanation of the Sabbath.

Sailors. No Retailer can recover Money of a Sailor, due for ſtrong Liquors.

Salt. Salt muſt be meaſured by an Officer in every Maritime Town, who is to have 17 *d. per* Hogſhead.

Seal. The Governour or Deputy muſt affix the publick Seal to all Commiſſions or publick Writings, without Fee.

The Secretary muſt write and get it ſeal'd for 1 *s.*

Self-murther. All Self-murtherers muſt be buried in the High way, with a Load of Stones on their Grave.

Schools, See **Miniſters.**

Sheep. Any Man may keep what Sheep he pleaſes on a Common not ſtinted, belonging to the Town where he he lives, on a Common ſtinted, he may uſe his Share, accounting five Sheep to a Cow.

The ſelect Men are to clear the Commons of Bruſh and Wood, and to ſet the Fines for putting Rams to the Flock.

Whoever moleſts Sheep, pays 5 *s.* and double Damages.

If a Dog kills or hurts Sheep, the Owner muſt hang him, or pay double Damages; if after Warning, he muſt do both.

Sheep muſt be waſh'd, and not put into dirty or ſandy Ground between that and ſheering, on penalty of 1 *s. per* Sheep.

No ſhort Locks or Lumps of Dirt or coarſe Tails to be wound in the Fleeces, on Penalty of 1 *s.*

Ship. The Owner or Builder of any new Ship muſt give Notice of it to the Governour, or his Deputy, or any two Magiſtrates before they plank, that Officers may view it, on penalty of 10 *l.*

The Surveyors may cauſe bad Materials to be chang'd; if the Builder and they differ, two Shipwrights ſwearing to be Faithful, muſt determine it, and be paid by him in Fault.

No Health to be drank on Board any Ship in Harbour, or Gun to be fir'd after Sunſet, or on the Sabbath, on penalty of 20 *s.* for every Health or Gun.

All Ships above 20 Tun, except thoſe whoſe Owners are Inhabitants, pay half a pound of Gun-powder for every Ton.

No Perſons are to trade with any Ship till it comes to Anchor, and under command.

Spinning. All Hands not employ'd, are oblig'd to ſpin.

The ſelect Men may aſſeſs Families at one fourth, half or whole Spinner, or more.

Every whole Spinner is to ſpin 3 pound *per* Week of Wollen, Cotton, or Linnen, for 30 Weeks in a Year, on penalty of 1 *s. per* pound ſhort.

Sodomy. Sodomy is puniſh'd with Death, if one of the Parties was forc'd, or under 14, ſhall not die, but be ſeverely puniſh'd.

Strangers. Chriſtian Strangers flying from Tyranny and Oppreſſion to be maintain'd by the publick 'till otherwiſe provided for. Men-

Men-Strangers upon their Arrival are to give an Account of themſelves before the Governour, or his Deputy, or two Magiſtrates, and to have the Benefit of, and to be ſubject to the Laws, as well as the Inhabitants.

None to be entertain'd above three Weeks without Licence, if the Conſtables know they are, they muſt return their Names to the County Court.

Strayers. Beaſts taken up ſtraying muſt be given to the Conſtable, and cry'd three Times, if worth 20 *s.* at the two next Markets, or meeting Houſes.

If the Finder gives no Notice in a Month, or records not the Goods found in three Months in the County Court, he forfeits the Value.

The Owner may claim in a Year, paying Charges, if no Claim be made, the Goods are half to the Finder, and half to the Country.

If they put not a Whith about the Neck of the Beaſt found ſtraying for a Month, they loſe the Charges of taking and keeping; if it be taken off by the Owner, he loſes the Value to the Finder.

No Beaſt is to be taken up as ſtraying, from the firſt of *April* to the 20th of *December*, unleſs it treſpaſs in Incloſures.

Sureties. Sureties for Appearance ſhall not be diſcharg'd 'till the Principal be ſurrendred, or the Execution ſatisfied, unleſs it be delay'd above a Month after Judgment.

Goods attached are held 'till Judgment is ſatisfied.

If Bond for Appearance is forfeited, the Court proceeds to Hearing and Judgment, and if the Plaintiff have a Verdict, Judgment is granted, and Execution iſſued againſt Defendants and Sureties.

Swearing. Whoever curſes or ſwears, pays 10 *s.* or ſits in the Stocks, if more than once, the Penalty is doubled.

Any Magiſtrate may determine this Cauſe.

Swine. The ſelect Men are to ſettle Orders, to prevent Miſchief by Swine, or to pay 40 *s.*

Satisfaction is to be made for the Damage they do, if the Fences were as the ſelect Men order'd.

If impounded, and not own'd for three Days, he may give three Days Notice to the two next Towns,

if

if within five miles, and ſell them by Outcry, or have them apprais'd, and keep them.

If the Owner appears, he may have the Overplus after Charges and Damages are defray'd.

T.

Tile-Earth. Tile-Earth muſt be dug before *November*, and turn'd once a month, on Penalty of half the Tiles made of that Earth.

Tobacco. None to ſmoak ſo near to a Houſe, Barn, *&c.* as to endanger firing it, on Penalty of 10 *l.* and Damages, if they happen.

None to ſmoke in a publick Houſe, ſo as to offend the maſter or gueſts, on Penalty of 2 *s.* 6 *d.*

Tolling of Cattle. All Cattle tolled muſt be tolled in the Clerk of the Writs Book, at 3 *s.* a Head, at the Peril of the Buyer.

The Seller enters his Name with two Vouchers, who are to make good the Damage, if the Cattle are challeng'd.

Any one who has loſt Cattle, may ſearch the Toll-Book without Charge.

Townſhip. The Freemen may make Laws for their Town, except in Criminal Caſes, and impoſe Fines under 20 *s.* and chuſe their ſelect men, not exceeding 9.

Any Houſholder aged 24, rated at 8 *l.* Eſtate, having taken the Oaths to the Government, may be a ſeect man, Juror, or Conſtable, though not free, provided the majority of ſelect men are ſo.

Every Town may fine one refuſing to ſerve as Conſtable 5 *l.* the Town of *Boſton* 10 *l.*

No Cottage or Dwelling-Houſe to be admitted to the Privilege of Common, but by the Towns Conſent.

Conſtables muſt ſerve the Warrants of the ſelect men, and levy their Fines.

Treaſurers. The County Treaſurer muſt keep exact Accounts, and not make any Payment to any indebted to the Country, without deducting the Debt.

All Fines ariſing in County Courts, or order'd by one Magiſtrate or Commiſſioner in Criminal Caſes are paid to him, the Treaſurer is choſen annually by the Freemen.

The

The Secretaries of Courts ſhall give an Account of all Dues coming to them within 14 Days after the Court ends, who is to warrant the Conſtable to levy them within a Week.

He is to give in his Account to the General Court every Year, and to have 1 *s. per* Pound for all Fines, and to be free from all Rates.

If he has not enough to defray publick Expences, the County Court muſt rate the County for the Deficiency.

He is to preſent the Names of negligent Conſtables to the County Court.

Tryals. All Tryals are by Bench and Jury, unleſs where the Law has order'd it otherwiſe.

An Offender may challenge any of his Jury, with ſhewing Cauſe.

Children and Ideots to have all reaſonable Allowances.

V.

Vagabonds. Vagabonds are to be carried before the Magiſtrate, and corrected, and ſent from Conſtable to Conſtable, 'till they come home, if they won't tell their Home, they go to the Houſe of Correction.

Votes. Every Freeman call'd to vote, may do it according to his Conſcience; if he is ſilent, he muſt be deem'd as a Negative.

If the Preſident of any Aſſembly will not put the Queſtion, the majority may, and puniſh him for refuſing.

Uſury. No man ſhall be adjudg'd for Forbearance of a Debt above 8 *per Cent. per Annum,* Bills of Exchange excepted.

W.

Watching. The Conſtable's Watch begins the firſt of *May*, and continues 'till *October*.

It muſt conſiſt of able men, and be order'd by the Conſtable, unleſs the ſelect men appoint otherwiſe.

All warn'd upon the Watch muſt ſerve, or pay 5 *s.* except remote Farmers, Magiſtrates, Deputies, Elders of Churches, Officers of the Country, or Militia.

The Watch muſt examine all in the Streets after 10, and ſecure them 'till morning, if they don't give a good Account of themſelves.

If

If any are found in Debauchery or Drunkeneſs, they are kept 'till the Law is ſatisfied.

Weights and Meaſures. The Treaſurer muſt provide, at the County's Charge, ſeal'd Meaſures and braſs Weights and Standards.

The Conſtable of every Town muſt get a Set try'd by theſe, and ſealed by the Treaſurer, or his Deputy.

He is to deliver them to the ſelect men; who are to chuſe an Officer to be ſworn in the next County Court, to whom all the Inhabitants are to bring their Weights and Meaſures to have them try'd, and ſeal'd the ſecond month in every Year.

The Conſtable, ſelect Men or Sealer pay 40 *s.* if they neglect their Duty, the Inhabitants 3 *s.* 4 *d.*

The ſelect Men muſt appoint one to be ſworn for meaſuring Corn, Wood, or Boards.

None are obliged to receive theſe Commodities, unleſs meaſur'd by him.

Wharfage. Goods are to pay Wharfage according to ſettled Rates, only where the Wharfs are made and maintain'd.

Weighty Goods muſt be ſet on End, or 7 Foot from the ſide, on Penalty of double Wharfage, none to lye on the Wharf above 48 Hours.

The Wharfinger may take his Wharfage out of the Goods, if not otherwiſe paid.

None to caſt Anchor, or do any thing elſe in, or near the *Cove* at *Boſton*, that may endanger other Veſſels, on Penalty of 10 *s.* beſides Damages.

None to caſt into the *Cove* any thing to fill it up, or annoy the Inhabitants, on Penalty of 40 *s.*

Wills. Wills muſt be recorded in the County Court, or Adminiſtration taken out within 30 Days after Demiſe.

Whoever enters upon, or embezzels the Eſtate of the Deceas'd, before he proves, and records the Will of the Deceas'd, or takes out Adminiſtration, pays all Debts of the Deceas'd, whether Aſſuits be prov'd, or not, and 5 *l. per* Month, 'till the Will is prov'd, or Adminiſtration taken out.

If an Executor refuſe to act, or Friends refuſe to adminiſter, the Clerk of the Writs in the Town, notifies it to the County Court, on Penalty of 40 *s. per* Month, and the Court takes Care of the Eſtate. Two

Two Magiſtrates with the Clerk of the County may take a Probate of Wills atteſted by two Witneſſes, or grant Adminiſtration, giving Notice of, and recording it in the next County Court.

The County Court divides the Eſtate of an Inteſtate among the Wife and Children; Daughters are to be Coheirs, and eldeſt Sons to have a double Portion.

Witches. Witches ſuffer Death.

Witneſſes. None to die but by two Evidences, *Viva Voce.*

Any Magiſtrate or Commiſſioner may take Evidence from one above 14, but it is not good in Court, unleſs the Perſon is preſent to be farther examin'd, except he live above 10 miles off, or is hindred by ſufficient Cauſe.

He who ſummons Witneſſes muſt pay their Charges, 2 *s. per* Day to thoſe 3 miles diſtant, and who are to paſs a Ferry, except that between *Charles-Town* and *Boſton*; 18 *d.* to others.

Whoever on the Tender of this refuſes to give in Evidence, pays the Party's Damages.

Witneſſes in Criminal Caſes are paid by the Treaſurers, and theſe by the Delinquents.

Wolves. Whoever kills a Wolf within 10 miles of a Plantation, contributing to the publick Charge, has 40 *s.*, 20 *s.* from the County, 10 *s.* from the Country, and 10 *s.* from the Town.

Wood. Wood brought by Water is aſſiz'd, at the Rate of three Load *per* 4 Ton.

Cordwood muſt be 8 Foot long, 4 high, and 4 broad, 1647.

Worſhip falſe. Idolatry is puniſh'd with Death after legal Conviction.

Wrecks. If any ſuffer Shipwreck, whether Friends or Enemies, their Perſons are to be harbour'd, and their Goods preſerv'd 'till farther Orders.

Whales, or other ſuch Fiſh driven on Shore, if they can't be kept ſhall be improv'd by the Townſhip, or Owners of the Land where they come on Shore, and an Account given to the next General Court.

Writs. All Writs, *&c.* are iſſued, and proceeded upon in the Name of the King, or Queen of *England.*

FINIS

Published by THE CARROLLTON PRESS.

Offset printed from the original

pages of the first edition

of 1720 and bound in

65 lb parchment

in the year

1991

AD

*